STRANGE ACCIDENT
OF STATE:

Henry VII and the Lambert Simnel Conspiracy

by

DAVID BEESTON

Lecturer in History
South Nottinghamshire College

First Published 1987

Published by David Beeston Esq.

Printed in Great Britain
Printed by Birchwood Publications, Somercotes, Derbys

I.S.B.N. 0 9512535 0 6

*'There followed this year, being the second of
the king's reign, a strange accident of state,
whereof the relations which we have are so
naked, that they leave it scarce credible;
not for the nature of it — for it hath fallen
out often — but for the manner and circumstances
of it, especially in the beginnings.'*

> Francis Bacon
> *'The History of the Reign of
> King Henry VII' (1622)*

HENRY VII: Unknown English artist, c. 1505-9.
Society of Antiquaries, London

CONTENTS

INTRODUCTION

This short work has two basic aims. First, it seeks to arouse interest in the Lambert Simnel conspiracy and the battle of Stoke Field which emanated from it in this, the year of its five hundredth anniversary. Secondly, it attempts — in a modest fashion — to help correct the misconceptions that the Wars of the Roses ended with the battle of Bosworth Field (August 22nd, 1485), and that Henry VII faced no serious military challenges after that date.

The commemoration of famous British battles and the growing awareness that their locations are a priceless part of our national heritage, have both been encouraging tendencies during recent years. In contrast with the last century, when the sites of several battlefields were built over, or bisected by railways, a more enlightened attitude has been in evidence of late, especially since the Second World War. Public interest in the nine hundredth anniversary of the battle of Hastings (1966), and the five hundredth anniversary of Bosworth (1985), has amply justified the time, effort, and money invested by both national and local government, as well as numerous voluntary organisations. Against this background, Stoke Field — a battle which many people in Britain have never even heard of, and which many more believe to be of minimal importance — certainly needs to be publicised more fully, and placed in its proper historical context.

For that to be attained, there is an urgent need to gain public acceptance of several crucial facts. This underrated, even denigrated, episode resulted in a major battle, in which more men participated than either Hastings or Bosworth. The victory of Henry VII at Stoke Field also had important political repercussions, for it resolved a serious threat to the new Tudor dynasty. It was not a minor, quixotic venture, formulated by eccentrics and incompetents; it was the last battle of the Wars of the Roses. The reasons why it was not accorded its true status at the time, were essentially political and partisan, but modern historians have increasingly felt no need to be constrained by these factors. Logically, there is no need for the general public to remain misinformed either.

It is definitely not my aim to devalue the battle of Bosworth Field or, for that matter, any other military actions which have taken place on British soil. Bosworth has a unique place in English history, all the more intriguing because of the long-standing controversy over the character and actions of Richard III. But Bosworth was not Henry VII's last battle, and it did not extinguish direct military challenges to his throne; the larger and more sanguinary conflict at Stoke Field, nearly two years later, has always held that position. Five hundred years later it is high time that this claim was finally acknowledged.

David Beeston
February, 1987

CHAPTER ONE

IN PLACE OF STRIFE

'England hath long been mad, and scarr'd herself;
The brother blindly shed the brother's blood,
The father rashly slaughter'd his own son,
The son, compell'd, been butcher to the sire:
All this divided York and Lancaster,
Divided in their dire division,
O, now, let Richmond and Elizabeth,
The true succeeders of each royal house,
By God's fair ordinance conjoin together!'

William Shakespeare
'King Richard III,' Act V, Scene V.

Two miles to the south of the small town of Market Bosworth in Leicestershire, lie the villages of Sutton Cheney and Shenton. Between them runs a ridge, approximately four hundred feet in height and just over a mile in length. Here, in the heart of the English midlands, the battle of Bosworth Field was fought and won by Henry Tudor, Earl of Richmond, on the morning of August 22nd, 1485.

Even by the standards of fifteenth century warfare, the battle had been a confused and unpredictable affair. Although Richmond's five thousand strong army had been out-numbered by two to one, his victory had been engineered by acts of treachery and crucial defections, in an encounter which lasted little more than two hours, and claimed barely a thousand lives. Yet this was the battle which led to the establishment of a new dynasty on the throne of England.

Richmond's defeated opponent, King Richard III, had been killed, and his mutilated body had been taken off to Leicester for an ignominious burial. Most of Richard's senior officers — including the Duke of Norfolk, Sir Robert Brackenbury, Sir Richard Ratcliffe, Lord Ferrers, and Sir William Catesby — had either perished in the fighting, or were executed soon afterwards. Before leaving the scene of his triumph, Richmond had been acclaimed as King Henry VII, and the reign of the first Tudor mcnarch had officially begun.

It has therefore been traditional to regard Bosworth Field as the last battle of the Wars of the Roses. These sporadic but bitter dynastic feuds between the rival Houses of York and Lancaster originated from the usurpation of Henry Bolingbroke, son of John of Gaunt, Duke of Lancaster, in 1399. By successfully deposing the tyrannical Richard II, and establishing himself as King Henry IV, he replaced the principle of natural succession with that of expediency. Thereafter, rebellions could easily be justified, whenever they were politically convenient.

During the reign of Henry IV (1399-1413) and that of his son, the all-conquering Henry V (1413-1422), the monarchy was relatively stable, but when the hero of Agincourt fell ill and died prematurely, leaving the throne to his nine month old son, Henry, problems quickly developed. The disastrous reign of Henry VI, witnessed the loss of virtually all English possessions in France by the end of the Hundred Years' War, and culminated with the King displaying unmistakable signs of insanity.

His logical replacement was the highly efficient and widely respected Richard, Duke of York, a great-grandson of Edward III, with a superior claim in his own right. Whilst Henry VI seemed unlikely to produce an heir, an uneasy compromise prevailed. York served loyally and patiently as Protector, with special responsibility for Ireland and Calais, and he and his sons would inherit the throne after Henry's death. However, the unexpected birth of the King's own son, Prince Edward, in October, 1453, encouraged the emergence of a powerful Lancastrian faction, dominated by Henry's warlike and indomitable Queen, Margaret of Anjou, who was determined that her child should not be disinherited. These developments appeared to extinguish Yorkist ambitions and in 1455 civil war erupted.

The Yorkists had gained a complete victory by 1461. Although Richard, Duke of York, had been killed in battle, his nineteen year old son, Edward IV, had routed the Lancastrians, confined the inert Henry VI in the Tower of London, and driven Margaret and her son abroad. Apart from one brief reversal (1470-71), Edward remained in control for the next twenty-two years.

His unforeseen death at the age of forty-one in April, 1483, precipitated a fresh crisis. Edward's twelve year old, son, Edward

V, reigned for less than three months before he and his younger brother, the nine year old Richard, Duke of York, were sent to the Tower by their ambitious and ruthless uncle, Richard, Duke of Gloucester, who proceeded to have both his nephews declared illegitimate by Parliament, and was himself crowned King Richard III in July, 1483.

Whether or not Richard sanctioned the murder of these helpless boys, is a complicated historical controversy which has not yet satisfactorily resolved. Indeed, Richard's reputation has been so thoroughly vilified over such a protracted period of time, that it is difficult to assess most aspects of his brief reign with the impartiality they deserve. On one issue, however, historians feel safe to make authoritative pronouncements. By 1484, Richard III was an unpopular monarch with many of his subjects, the target of evil rumours and conspiracies, of which the Duke of Buckingham's abortive rebellion in October was the most serious. Increasingly, those who were disenchanted with Richard, transferred their loyalty to Henry Tudor, Earl of Richmond, currently exiled in Brittany.

Richmond had spent half of his twenty-eight years abroad, but he was the strongest surviving claimant available to the battered House of Lancaster. From his father, Edmund Tudor, and his mother, Lady Margaret Beaufort, he was a direct descendant of both the English and French royal families, and as a Welshman, born at Pembroke Castle and besieged in Harlech for seven years, he was assured of strong regional support. When he landed near Milford Haven on August 7th, 1485, accompanied by a party of exiled friends and two thousand French mercenaries, he was able to attract enough support to triumph over the inactive and disloyal forces of Richard III, and win himself the crown.

The new king arrived in London on September 3rd, twelve days after Bosworth Field, and was warmly received at Shoreditch by the Lord Mayor and Aldermen. After all, Henry's predecessor had been unpopular in the capital on account of the forced loans he had exacted to finance his military campaigns in 1484 and 1485. Furthermore, the conspiracies and uncertainty surrounding the childless Richard III had hardly created the political stability on which commercial growth could be firmly based.

Despite these greetings, Henry VII was highly sensitive to the inherent weakness of his position. The array of rival claimants in the defeated Yorkist camp was positively daunting. Among the

THE HOUSE OF LANCASTER

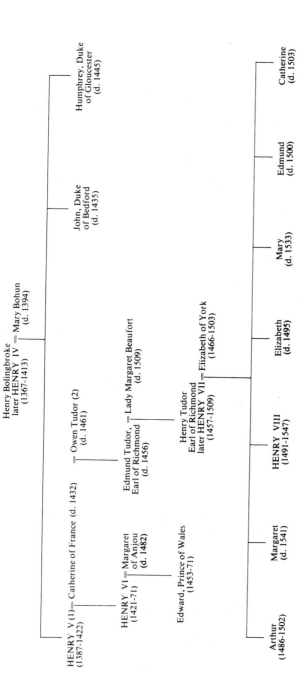

Henry Bolingbroke
later HENRY IV = Mary Bohun
(1367-1413)   (d. 1394)

Humphrey, Duke
of Gloucester
(d. 1445)

John, Duke
of Bedford
(d. 1435)

HENRY V (1) = Catherine of France (d. 1432)
(1387-1422)

= Owen Tudor (2)
(d. 1461)

Edmund Tudor, = Lady Margaret Beaufort
Earl of Richmond   (d. 1509)
(d. 1456)

Henry Tudor
Earl of Richmond
later HENRY VII = Elizabeth of York
(1457-1509)   (1466-1503)

HENRY VI = Margaret
(1421-71)   of Anjou
                 (d. 1482)

Edward, Prince of Wales
(1453-71)

Arthur
(1486-1502)

Margaret
(d. 1541)

HENRY VIII
(1491-1547)

Elizabeth
(d. 1495)

Mary
(d. 1533)

Edmund
(d. 1500)

Catherine
(d. 1503)

THE HOUSE OF YORK

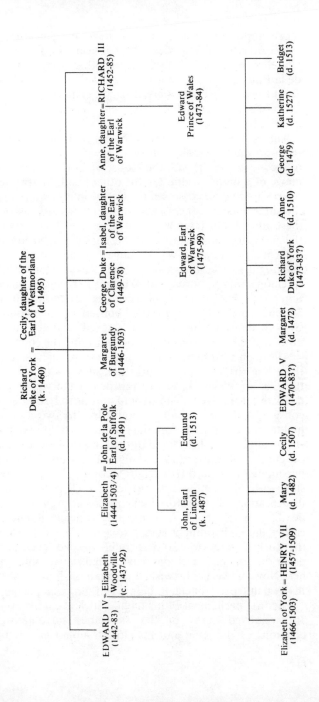

more important, were three nephews of Edward IV. One was Edward, Earl of Warwick, the ten-year old son of the Duke of Clarence, Edward IV's brother; the others were John and Edmund de la Pole, the young sons of Edward IV's sister, Elizabeth. Apart from these male contenders, Henry's claim was also weakened by Edward's five surviving daughters, including his own fiancée, Elizabeth of York.

Throughout the first year of his reign, Henry's approach to this problem was essentially contradictory. On the one hand, he sought to reconcile himself with the House of York, if only to present the image of a united realm. On the other hand, he was determined to emphasise that he possessed the throne in his own right, and not on the sufferance of others. The inevitable acts of discourtesy which these attitudes fostered would cause great offence to many influential and dangerous members of the Yorkist establishment.

Henry's coronation was organised without delay by Sir Robert Willoughby, the Steward of the Royal Household, and the ceremony was performed at Westminster Abbey on Sunday, October 30th, by Thomas Bourchier, the Archbishop of Canterbury. Simultaneously, the King busied himself by augmenting the Council with many of his own hand-picked advisers, and by placing other trusted supporters in key posts around the country.

Although Elizabeth of York had been brought south to London from Sherriff Hutton in Yorkshire, along with her young cousin the Earl of Warwick, Henry postponed the wedding for the immediate future. He had no wish to appear to be a king by his wife's consent, and was probably grateful for the two legal niceties that had to be cleared up before the ceremony could take place. Firstly, she would have to be cleared of the taint of bastardy imposed upon the children of Edward IV and his wife, Elizabeth Woodville, at the beginning of Richard III's reign. Secondly, Henry's blood relationship with his fiancée was sufficiently close to require a Papal dispensation. He therefore had convenient excuses to delay his impending marriage. As a vulnerable exile at Rennes, two years earlier, he had willingly agreed to a match which would give him the Yorkist support he so desperately needed, even though he had never met the girl, and may have only briefly communicated with her. Now, however, he wished to establish himself as a king with his own independent claim, before fulfilling that pledge.

The first parliament of his reign, which assembled on November 7th, removed many of the anomalies surrounding the legal positions of the King and his closest supporters. A brief Act of

Confirmation recognised Henry's claim to the throne, by right of succession and victory in battle. His future mother-in-law, Elizabeth Woodville, was restored to her previous dignity of Queen Dowager, and all her children were cleared of the stigma of illegitimacy. Lady Margaret Beaufort, his own mother, regained all her estates as Countess of Richmond and Derby, which had been confiscated by Richard III in 1483, and became henceforth one of the wealthiest women in England. Finally, the Acts of Attainder, which had proclaimed the former Earl of Richmond and many other Lancastrians as traitors, were reversed upon the dead King Richard III and more than twenty of his confederates, though a general pardon issued earlier promised general clemency to those among his former enemies who would submit to his authority.

Even though his position was immeasurably strengthened by this legislation, Henry had to be urged by parliament itself to proceed with his marriage. On December 11th, Sir Thomas Lovell, the Speaker, presented the King with a petition from the Commons, seconded by the Lords, suggesting that the wedding should take place without furter delay. The permission of Pope Innocent VIII had been communicated through his Papal Legate, the Bishop of Imola, and the ceremony was finally performed on January 18th, 1486.

Having appeased the House of York by removing one potential grievance, the King soon presented it with another. The coronation of his wife, which many assumed would be a logical corollary of the wedding, became the subject of further vexatious delays. Elizabeth was soon pregnant. Indeed, she had almost certainly been living with her future husband before their marriage. Once again, Henry had a convenient excuse to postpone a ceremony which he felt would detract from his personal status. Instead, he spent the early months of 1486 on a Royal Progress of the North and Midlands, crushing minor Yorkist revolts in Yorkshire and Worcestershire, and generally making himself known, before arriving back in London in June.

He did not stay long in the capital. Ever conscious of the value of propaganda, he had decided that his first child should be born at a location that would strengthen the Tudor claim to the throne. Before the end of the month, he and his wife had set off for Winchester, the former capital of Wessex, and in this venerable city their first son was born on September 20th. Typically, the infant prince was named Arthur, inferring an unbroken line of descent between the Tudors and the most exalted of the ancient British kings.

The baby's christening in Winchester Cathedral was the occasion for a remarkable outward display of harmony. The pro-Lancastrian Earls of Oxford and Derby both acted as god-fathers to the child, though the House of York was even more heavily represented. Prince Arthur was carried by his aunt Cecily, the second daughter of Edward IV; his godmother was Elizabeth, the Queen Dowager, Edward's widow; and two other Yorkist noblemen, John de la Pole, Earl of Lincoln, and Thomas Grey, Marquess of Dorset, were also in attendance.

When this important formality had been successfully concluded, Henry took his wife and child back to the royal palace at Greenwich, where they kept the feast of All Hallows, and later celebrated Christmas. No doubt he felt well-satisfied with events during the first year of his reign. He had little cause to be, for he had made important mistakes.

The worst of these was his failure to fully reconcile the House of York. Even after his deferred marriage, and the birth of a son and heir, there were no immediate plans afoot for his wife's coronation. This second snub rendered him vulnerable to the allegations of self-interest and opportunism. Unpleasant comparisons were soon being drawn between Henry VII and Richard III. The Princes in the Tower had not been seen since the summer of 1483, shortly after Richard's accession; the young Earl of Warwick had similarly disappeared into the Tower during the autumn of 1485, soon after Henry's triumphant entry into London.

Widespread conjectures that young Warwick had died of natural causes, or had been murdered, or had escaped, did not worry Henry unduly. Secretive by nature, he failed to realise that his own silence was actually encouraging the scandal-mongers. Early in the new year, he would be rudely awakened by a well-planned and highly dangerous conspiracy, which rebuked his complacency with terrifying speed.

CHAPTER TWO

A TANGLED WEB

'Latest among such adventurers was a lowborn
priest called Richard, whose surname was Simons,
a man as cunning as he was corrupt. He evolved
a villainous deed of this sort, by which he might
trouble the country's tranquillity.'

Polydore Vergil
'Anglica Historia'. (1534)

The tactical errors made by Henry VII became increasingly evident after the November of 1486. Rumours began to circulate that more would soon be heard of the Earl of Warwick, and barely two months later an imposter, purporting to be this young claimant to the throne, arrived in Ireland. The pretender's name was undoubtedly Lambert Simnel. In most other respects, though, precise details about the boy are lacking, and the few confused facts available suggest an ignorance on the part of government officials and chroniclers alike.

He probably originated from Oxford where his father, reputedly named Thomas Simnel, worked as a skilled craftsman, in one of several occupations. The word "Simnel", in Middle English, was used to describe a small cake or bun, made from fine, flour, which was boiled, then baked, and proved popular during the Christmas, Easter, and Mid-Lent festivities. On this basis, it had been claimed that Simnel's father was himself a baker, though other suggestions include shoe-maker, tailor, organ-maker, and joiner. Simnel's exact age at the time of the crisis in which he would be involved, is also unknown, with contemporary estimates ranging from ten to fifteen. Logically, he would probably have been about twelve years old, this being the age of the subject he would be required to impersonate.

Simnel has correctly been dismissed by both his contempories, and by modern historians, as a pathetic pawn in the hands of older, unscrupulous political figures. Nevertheless, there can be little doubt that he displayed several important attributes, many of which were remarkable in someone of his age and social background. An attractive physical appearance, graceful movements, intelligence, adaptability, and a natural air of dignity, all helped to produce an uncanny ability to impersonate others of a higher social standing.

These were the qualities which, probably by the age of ten, had brought him to the attention of a twenty-eight year old priest named Richard or William Symonds, who was then studying at Oxford. This cunning and manipulative character disappeared into lifelong imprisonment after the events in which he played a minor, but initially important role, and consequently little is known about him. It is clear, however, that his motives were dominated by self-interest. Filled with illusions of grandeur, this man of humble origins had dreamt that he was the tutor to a king, and saw his young protégé as a means of ingratiating himself upon the defeated Yorkists. The elevation of the recently-exiled Bishop John Morton to the position of Archbishop of Canterbury in 1486, showed how instant personal advancement could be attained by aiding the victors in a volatile political situation.

Symonds had therefore established contact with disgruntled Yorkists, probably projecting Simnel as a future child-king, buttressed by their political and military power. The actual supporters of this conspiracy are not fully known, but two of the main collaborators can be identified beyond reasonable doubt.

The first, and most important was Henry VII's mother-in-law, Elizabeth, the Queen Dowager. Now nearly fifty years old, this erratic and unpredictable woman had seldom been far from the political centre of gravity during the previous twenty-three years. As Elizabeth Woodville, the young and beautiful widow of a Lancastrian knight, Sir John Grey, killed at the second battle of St. Albans (1461), she had appealed to Edward IV in 1464 for the restoration of her husband's lands. Consumed with passion, Edward had married her soon after, and during the next nineteen years they produced ten children, of whom seven (two sons and five daughters) reached maturity. In addition, Elizabeth's many relatives received social and political advancement, and became an integral part of the Yorkist state.

The death of her husband in 1483, followed by the removal, and possible murder, of her sons at the hands of her brother-in-law, Richard III, had led her to conspire herself on behalf of the Lancastrian Earl of Richmond in 1484 and 1485. After his victory and accession as Henry VII, her eldest daughter, Elizabeth had married him, as we have already seen, and outwardly the Queen Dowager appeared to have accepted the new son-in-law whom she had helped install as king. He, in turn, had repaid her support and co-operation, by restoring her dower lands, which belonged to the Duchy of Lancaster, in March, 1486, under the authority of the Great Seal of England.

Behind this facade of cordiality, she nursed an important personal grievance. Her daughter had not been crowned as Queen, even after the birth of Prince Arthur, and clearly Henry VII did not acknowledge that his wife was of any political significance in the Tudor administration. He had merely used the marriage to display a spirit of reconciliation, weakening the House of York's claim to the throne, whilst doing nothing practical to accommodate their political aspirations. The Queen Dowager had already shown herself to be a dangerous enemy to those who jeopardized her family's interests, as the King knew only too well. It was in her withdrawing chamber that the successful conspiracy against Richard III had been initiated. Not surprisingly, she was to become Henry's prime suspect after Simnel's appearance in Ireland.

A second conspirator who was almost certainly prepared to avail himself of Simnel and Symonds, was the implacable Yorkist nobleman, Viscount Francis Lovell. Barely thirty years of age, Lovell may have been Richard III's best friend, and definitely had been one of the pillars of his short-lived regime. This energetic member of the Yorkist party, had first entered royal service during the last years of Edward IV's reign, and had been knighted by Richard, then Duke of Gloucester, during an expedition to Scotland in 1480, which had resulted in the capture of Berwick-on-Tweed. Soon after, Lovell had been created a Viscount in January, 1483. Following the death of the king, just three months later, he had transferred his allegiance to Richard III, a leader he knew and respected, in preference to the inexperienced Edward V. If he had also expected to be rewarded for lending his support to Richard, then he was not disappointed. He had acted as his Lord Chamberlain, had helped him to suppress Buckingham's rebellion in 1484, and had served loyally under him amidst the treachery on Bosworth Field. Lovell had been one of the few survivors from Richard's Household, and had escaped after the defeat and death of his master.

Accompanied by two other prominent Yorkists, Humphrey and

Thomas Stafford, he had taken sanctuary at St. John's in Colchester during the winter of 1485-86, though he regarded this as a mere expedient. In the spring of 1486, abandoning his temporary refuge, he had attempted to organise a rebellion, centred upon the Yorkist stronghold at Middleham in North Yorkshire, to coincide with another led by the Staffords in Worcestershire. Both ventures had quickly collapsed, and the Staffords had been arrested. Once again, though Lovell remained at large. Hiding first in Lancashire, where he was protected by his powerful Yorkist friend and sympathiser, Sir Thomas Broughton, and later near Ely in the Fens, he remained a thorn in the side of Henry VII, whom he naturally regarded as a hated usurper. Lovell's sudden departure for Flanders, early in 1487, was therefore a strong indication of his involvement in, or even his instigation of, this latest attempt to unseat the king.

Originally, the Queen Dowager, Viscount Lovell, and the other anonymous supporters of this embryonic rebellion, had planned to train their new-found acquisition, Lambert Simnel, to impersonate Richard, Duke of York, the younger son of Edward IV. This choice was soon abandoned, however, in favour of the Earl of Warwick, and by changing to this alternative claimant, the conspirators gained important tactical advantages.

The Duke of York had not been seen outside the Tower for nearly three and a half years, and was generally presumed dead. Even if he was still alive, both he and his elder brother, Edward V, had been declared illegitimate by parliament at the beginning of Richard III's reign (June 26th, 1483), and although this had recently been reversed by Henry VII's first parliament, the boy's origins had been tarnished. By comparison, the Earl of Warwick bore no such stigma, and was more morally acceptable as a future king. Although his father, the Duke of Clarence, had been attainted before his death in 1478, this might be seen as the lesser of two evils in an age when Acts of Attainder were common enough.

Furthermore, the Earl of Warwick was, deservedly, an object of popular sympathy. Orphaned at the age of three, after the execution of his father, and the murder of his mother (who had been poisoned by household servants), Warwick had been brought up in claustrophobic and oppressive conditions. Under the supervision of his aunt, Anne, Duchess of Gloucester, until her death in March, 1485, and her husband, later King Richard III, the boy had been strictly confined in Middleham and Sherriff Hutton castles, in Yorkshire.

His miserable lot had not improved under Henry VII. After the victory at Bosworth Field, Henry had realised only too well the political importance of this pathetic and ill-used child. Before even departing from Leicester, he had despatched the trusted Sir Robert Willoughby to Sherriff Hutton. Willoughby carried the King's warrant, instructing the constable of the castle to hand over Elizabeth of York, Henry's fiancée, and the ten year-old Earl, both of whom had been quickly conveyed to London. Warwick was immediately accommodated in the Tower, where — with the exception of one day's liberty — he would spend the remaining fourteen years of his wretched existence. Cut off from normal social relationships, and denied contact with everyday objects, he almost inevitably became mentally subnormal, and it was commonly believed that "he could not discern a goose from a capon". By continuing the incarceration of this unfortunate boy, Henry had sullied his own image, and given a useful propaganda weapon to unreconciled Yorkists.

The rumours which were circulating by the end of 1486 that young Warwick was no longer alive and well in the Tower, made it expedient for the conspirators to alter Simnel's imposture. If these tales proved correct, then Warwick could not be produced by Henry VII to undermine Simnel's claim. Alternatively, if the King tried to admit that his prisoner had died or escaped, he personally risked being vilified as a child murderer in the mould of Richard III, with a further loss of public support.

Having therefore decided that Simnel would impersonate the Earl of Warwick, his mentors put their plan into operation. In January, 1487, accompanied by his tutor-priest, Symonds, the pretender sailed for Ireland. Their immediate tasks were to make contact with the powerful Yorkist establishment there, convince them of the boy's authenticity, and establish a secure base for the invasion of England.

CHAPTER THREE

SUCCESS IN IRELAND

> *'The king had been a little improvident in the
> matters of Ireland, and had not removed officers
> and counsellors, and put in their places, or at
> least intermingled, persons of whom he stood
> assured. This he should have done, since he
> knew the strong bent of that country towards
> the House of York, and that it was a ticklish
> and unsettled state, more easy to receive
> distempers and mutations than England was.'*

*Francis Bacon
'The History of the Reign of
King Henry VII'. (1622)*

England's long and strife-torn intervention in Ireland had begun more than three hundred years earlier. In 1169 a strong force commanded by Richard le Clare, Earl of Pembroke (nicknamed "Strongbow") had landed there, and launched the campaigns which forcibly united the country with the English Crown.

Over the centuries two distinct political entities had developed. On the east coast, a small anglicised enclave had been established, roughly thirty miles long by twenty miles wide, and known as the Pale. This stronghold of English influence was separated from the rest of the country by an earth bank and palisade. Its capital, Dublin, was the seat of an autonomous Irish parliament, which had evolved by the end of the 13th century.

Beyond the Pale, in the less-developed rural areas, administrative control was maintained by a small number of powerful Anglo-Irish families, through a series of Earldoms. By the end of the 15th century, the most important were the Fitz Geralds, who held the Earldoms of Kildare and Desmond, and the Butlers, who held the Earldom of Ormond. The relationship of these provincial magnates with the people they governed was more complex than in England. In both countries, the traditional feudal tie still existed. The Earls owned the land which the serfs farmed, and exacted the same traditional dues in return. But in Ireland, the remoteness of many areas from strong central authority gave the ruling families an aura of kingship at local level, and engendered fierce, tribal loyalties, which often ignored the dictates of national government.

The House of York had consistently exploited this political autonomy for more than thirty years. Richard, Duke of York, had been appointed Lord Lieutenant of Ireland in December, 1447. During his two periods of residence there (July, 1449 to September, 1450 and October, 1454 to July, 1460) he had impressed the local nobility as a benevolent ruler. Needing a secure haven when preparing his rebellion against Henry VI, he had deemed it an act of high treason to bring any writs, privy seals or commandments over from England. To the great Anglo-Irish families, who were increasingly impatient of interference from England (and had the example of an independent Scotland close at hand), this legal device was most welcome. Richard of York, and his sons, Edward IV and Richard III, were all highly regarded by the powerful Fitz Gerald family, who were now in the ascendant. Within a year of Edward IV's victories in England (1461), the Fitz Geralds had militarily crushed the pro-Lancastrian Butler family. After that, the seventh and eighth Earls of Kildare (both Fitz Geralds) successively held the post of Lord Deputy, or Viceroy, and from Dublin Castle they loyally upheld Yorkist authority for the next twenty-three years.

The overthrow of the House of York in 1485 initially had little effect in Ireland. Before dismantling the Yorkist administration there, Henry VII had to find efficient substitutes. Given the disarray of his natural allies, the Butlers, that could not be achieved immediately. Their nominal head, the seventh Earl of Ormond, had spent little time in Ireland, and political leadership of the family was in dispute between rival branches. So ineffective had the Butlers become as an opposition group, that the seventh Earl had even seemed willing to reach a compromise with the House of York during the reign of Richard III.

Henry VII could not easily reverse this situation, though he had tried to restore the Butlers' status. The Earl of Ormond had been admitted to the King's Council, and appointed as Chamberlain to the Queen. For the time being, though, the Fitz Geralds held sway in Ireland. Gerald Fitz Gerald, the eighth Earl of Kildare, remained in his post of Lord Deputy, and his brother, Thomas, continued as Lord Chancellor. These pro-Yorkist dignitaries were the best hope of succour for the conspirators in England.

When Simnel and Symonds arrived in Dublin in January, 1487, the latter probably contacted the Lord Deputy at once, and arranged a private audience. At this meeting, Symonds convinced the Earl of Kildare that the boy was indeed the Earl of Warwick, whom he had rescued from certain death in the Tower of London. This spurious claim was aided substantially by Simnel's dignified, yet natural, behaviour. Kildare privately disseminated this information to many other members of the Anglo-Irish nobility, and found widespread support for the recognition of the boy's claim to the throne. The Duke of Clarence had actually been born in Dublin in 1449, and the arrival of his young son, a grand-child of the fondly-remembered Richard, Duke of York, was an emotional event. However, before acknowledging his claim publicly they had to gain a broad popular consent. Therefore, rumours of young Warwick's escape and arrival in Ireland were circulated, and to the satisfaction of the Fitz Geralds the public clamoured for action. Quite apart from their longstanding affection for the House of York, many were excited by the prospect of placing their own protégé on the throne of their mighty neighbour — the same impulse which had rallied several thousand Welshmen to the Earl of Richmond, two years earlier.

The niceties of the right of succession, which were of great importance in England, were mere legal quibbles to the Irish. The attainder of the Earl of Warwick's father, Clarence, counted for little, especially since the recent success of Henry Tudor had demonstrated that such acts did not prevent the crown passing from one king to another. Nor did the existence of Edward IV's five daughters bother the Irish in the least; their rights had been completely ignored by Richard III, and they were now deemed to be in the clutches of Henry VII, entirely against their will.

With no legal impediments to delay his progress, the pretender Simnel was installed in Dublin Castle, and within a few days he had been proclaimed as King Edward VI. Although his coronation was to be deferred for the present, the Yorkist conspirators had nevertheless achieved a dramatic breakthrough. They now controlled the Irish capital and seat of government, from which their military and diplomatic manoeuvres could be undertaken. By the end of January, as their agents began arriving in England and on the Continent, to circulate news of the rebellion's progress, an alarmed

Henry VII was forced to consider what measures he would use to contain this latest challenge to his authority.

CHAPTER FOUR

THE COUNCIL OF SHEEN

'Accordingly a council of nobles having been
summoned at the Carthusians' convent at the
royal palace which the king later called
Richmond, the remedies appropriate to the
dangerous condition were debated.'

Polydore Vergil
'Anglica Historia'. (1534)

The success of Simnel and Symonds did not pose an immediate threat to Henry VII's rule in England. Nevertheless, the King reacted with the energy and firmness which characterised his response to many other rebellions, both before and after the present crisis.

On February 2nd, he held a meeting of his Council in the Carthusian charter-house, close to the royal residence at Sheen, on the south bank of the Thames. This building, which had been erected by Henry V more than seventy years earlier, was an ideal venue for proceedings which were urgent and confidential.

Henry VII's Council had a potential membership of about two hundred, consisting of noblemen, clerics, lawyers and country gentlemen, but in practice he availed himself of only a small group of them at any one meeting, the most common number being seven. Those present at the Council of Sheen included John Morton, the Archbishop of Canterbury; Richard Fox, the King's Secretary and Lord Privy Seal; and John de la Pole, the young Earl of Lincoln. All were politically-experienced advisers whom he felt he could trust. In keeping with the personality of Henry VII, the proceedings were "closed" (i.e. secret), and the conclusions drawn by the King and his councillors can only be gauged in the light of their subsequent actions.

It is obvious that the Queen Dowager was held to be largely responsible for the incipient rebellion. Immediately after the Council meeting, she was accused of disloyalty to the King (then the Earl of Richmond) nearly three years earlier, when she had appeared to reach a compromise with Richard III.

On that occassion, in March, 1484, she had been trapped with her five surviving daughters in the sanctuary of Westminster, and had agreed to terminate this unhappy state of affairs by submitting to Richard. He, in turn, had promised to provide for her generously, and find suitable husbands for the young ladies. As Henry VII well knew, this had been a cynical arrangement on both sides. Richard III had made the offers to persuade the former Queen to abandon all hope of foreign aid, and force her to withdraw the promise she had made to the Earl of Richmond that he could marry her eldest daughter, Elizabeth. She had been equally pragmatic. Since Richard was only thirty-two years old, remaining in sanctuary with her daughters presented an irksome, if not interminable prospect, even if he had not ended it by force, which was by no means improbable. Therefore, her compromise in 1484, which was now dredged up at Sheen, had been no more than an act of real-politik. Moreover, it had not prevented her from conspiring against Richard III, on behalf of Henry Tudor, during the Buckingham Rebellion of 1484, and the successful invasion of 1485. Clearly, this dated and unconvincing allegation against the Queen Dowager was a mere excuse. Her involvement in the new conspiracy was Henry's real concern.

Her punishments, when weighed against her age, social position, and relationship to the King, were most severe. All her lands and estates were confiscated, without any legal proceedings, and settled upon her daughter, Elizabeth, Henry's wife. Without private means, the Queen Dowager was sent as a virtual prisoner to Bermondsey Abbey where, as Edward IV's widow, she was entitled to the use of several apartments. The pension of four hundred marks, which her son-in-law bestowed upon her, was very modest and although it was slightly increased three years later, there can be little doubt that she lived "a wretched and miserable life"(Hall) during the remaining five years at Bermondsey, making only a single public appearance. Shortly before her death in June, 1492, she would pathetically claim in her will that she had no worldly goods. In asking to be buried at Windsor, beside her husband, she bitterly expressed a desire that this should be performed speedily, and with little pomp — requests to which Henry VII acceded.

Draconian measures against his erring mother-in-law were not the only matters discussed at Sheen. It was also decided that a public appearance by the real Earl of Warwick was urgently needed to inflict severe damage on Simnels's bogus claim. On the following Sunday, the boy was taken from the Tower and led through the centre of London to St. Paul's Cathedral. Here he prayed and worshipped at High Mass, and afterwards was allowed to speak to many important people who knew him personally, including members of the Council which had been in convocation that day. This ploy was most effective in England, as would later be revealed by strong, popular support for Henry VII, and considerable reservations about Simnel's identity. In Ireland, however, circumstances were different. There, the pro-Yorkist political establishment had already committed itself, and it was too late for them to turn back. They were not in the least impressed by news of this public exhibition. On the contrary, they attempted to turn Henry's action against him, accusing the King of profanity for using a holy place to embellish his own impostor.

Finally, Henry's Council made two other important proclamations. A pardon was offered to all offenders in England, including those guilty of high treason, this being a clear reference to men like Sir Thomas Broughton, who were already collaborating with the conspirators. Furthermore, all sea ports were to be closely watched to prevent any potential supporters of Simnel from joining the pretender, swelling the rebel forces and boosting their morale.

All these measures were indicative of the seriousness with which Henry VII and his advisers were treating the unexpected developments in Ireland. Their desire to nip them in the bud was manifest. But if they thought that their swift riposte might deal the rebellion a fatal blow, they were sadly mistaken. Within a few weeks, the conspirators would be reinforced and heartened by the acquisition of an experienced and forceful leader, from among the ranks of the King's Council itself.

CHAPTER FIVE

THE DEFECTION OF THE EARL OF LINCOLN

> *'For in England they won to their party John,*
> *Earl of Lincoln, son of John de la Pole, Duke*
> *of Suffolk and of Elizabeth, King Edward the*
> *Fourth's eldest sister. This Earl was a man*
> *of great wit and courage, and had his thoughts*
> *highly raised by hopes and expectations for a*
> *time.'*
>
> Francis Bacon
> *'The History of the Reign of*
> *King Henry VII' (1622)*

Few, if any, contemporary Englishmen had acquired the same breadth of administrative experience, at so early an age, as John de la Pole, Earl of Lincoln. Although he was no more than twenty-five years old, he had held several of the highest offices in the realm for nearly four years, under both Richard III and Henry VII. His proven worth as a statesman, combined with his own unique claim to the throne, had produced a dynamic young nobleman, who could be regarded by his reigning monarch as either a valued supporter or a dangerous potential enemy.

The son of the elder John de la Pole, Earl of Suffolk, and Elizabeth, the sister of Edward IV and Richard III, Lincoln had been born sometime between 1462 and 1464. He had grown to adulthood during the reigns of both his uncles, and had naturally derived considerable benefits from the almost unbroken period of Yorkist hegemony which had begun shortly before his birth. Whilst still a child he had been created Earl of Lincoln in March, 1467, and a Knight of the Bath in April, 1475. Eight years later, now a young man mourning the death of a beloved relative, he had attended Edward IV's funeral.

However, it was during the brief reign of his tragic younger cousin, Edward V, (April to June, 1483), that his political

markedly. His support was quickly secured
e, Richard, Duke of Gloucester, and sym-
the orb at the coronation of the new King
7th, 1483. This gesture from Lincoln marked
ɔ years of heady success. Within weeks, he had
esident (later Lieutenant) of the Council of the
erriff Hutton castle in Yorkshire.

advancements soon followed. In April, 1484,
ant son Edward had died at Middleham, and since
his wife, ___ Anne, suffered from permanent ill-health and was
unlikely to bear more children, a successor to the king had to be
nominated. Richard's first choice was his younger nephew, the Earl
of Warwick, Clarence's son, then just nine years old; but he soon
reversed this decision in favour of Lincoln. Here was an older and
more substantial claimant who, unlike Warwick, did not have the
liability of an attainted father, and could immediately be prepared
for his future duties. Logically, he received the additional appoint-
ment of Lord Lieutenant of Ireland in August, 1484.

Material success accompanied this dramatic rise in status. As heir
to the throne, he was awarded a pension of £176 a year. Furthermore, he was assured that the estates of Lady Margaret Beaufort
would revert to him after the death of her third husband, Lord
Thomas Stanley; since Richard III had no intention of allowing
these lands to pass on to her son, the exiled Earl of Richmond, this
was an inexpensive way of rewarding a supporter and disinheriting
an enemy.

By the end of Richard's brief reign, Lincoln had already earned a
formidable reputation. Serious, courageous and intelligent, his
nickname was "the Dark Earl" and having survived the battle of
Bosworth Field, his future caused Henry VII considerable soul-
searching. Sparing a rival claimant was not a decision to be taken
lightly, but — on balance — it seemed the wiser course of action.
An execution or indefinite period of imprisonment would have
alienated Lincoln's influential family, and would further tarnish
the reputation of the new king, which was by no means spotless after his incarceration of the young Earl of Warwick in the Tower. It
seemed more advisable to leave Lincoln at liberty as a co-rival to
the boy, thus dividing potential Yorkist opposition. Nevertheless,
Henry took the obvious precaution of having him secretly watched.

Outwardly, Lincoln accepted his new master and seemed willing
to co-operate with him. Accompanied by his father, he had attended the first parliament of Henry's reign in November, 1485, and

the following July they were appointed as justices of oyer and terminer, required to deal with cases of murder, conspiracy, treason and unlawful assembly in the city of London and its suburbs. He continued to serve on the King's Council, and was present at Sheen, and at St. Paul's when the Earl of Warwick was exhibited. Yet, a short time later, at the beginning of Lent, he deserted Henry and escaped to the Continent with the intention of joining, and indeed strengthening, the incipient rebellion.

It is not impossible, that Lincoln had been involved in the conspiracy from the outset. After all, he certainly had contacts in Ireland, to where Simnel and Symonds were sent. On balance, though it seems far more likely that he only joined the rebellion after its inception, having been influenced by correspondence from his aunt, Margaret of Burgundy, who would soon become one of its principal supporters.

Lincoln's sudden defection was more than just a startling and hurtful act of betrayal to Henry VII; it was also a confusing, if not mysterious, affair for which a wholly convincing explanation has never been formulated. Having recently seen the true Earl of Warwick, he knew that Simnel was an impostor, yet he was still prepared to support this bogus claimant before friend and foe alike. Personal ambition may have been the cause. Once Simnel had served his purpose and had been discreetly removed, Lincoln himself would be an obvious alternative, acceptable to Yorkists everywhere. Self-preservation could also have influenced his decision, for if he stayed in England he risked being unjustly accused of supporting the rebels, whether innocent or not. He was, after all, a marked man already.

A more elaborate theory suggests that the real aim of the conspiracy was to re-establish on the throne one of Edward IV's young sons, who had — in some unspecified manner — survived, and escaped from the Tower, but was himself too valuable to risk at the head of a hazardous military venture, until it had actually succeeded. Certainly, this objective would have elicited the support of most of those leading Yorkists who backed the conspiracy to the hilt, including the Queen Dowager, Viscount Lovell, Margaret of Burgundy, and the Earl of Lincoln himself. It is not, therefore, an unreasonable analysis, but in the absence of firm evidence, it must remain purely a matter of conjecture.

If Lincoln's motives were vague, his immediate intentions were clear enough. He headed for the court of his aunt Margaret, Duchess of Burgundy. This formidable woman, with her passionate Yorkist sympathies, could be guaranteed to give the rebels all the practical help at her disposal.

Margaret was the younger sister of Lincoln's mother, Elizabeth. Since becoming the third wife of Charles the Bold, Duke of Burgundy, in 1468 she had lived largely on the Continent, but had still rejoiced in the fortunes of her brothers, Edward IV and Richard III, and deeply resented the discomfiture of the House of York in 1485. This sentiment was reinforced by a strong personal dislike of Henry VII. She never forgave her niece, Elizabeth of York, for marrying him and thereby strengthening his position, and she remained one of his most irreconcilable enemies, who generously supported all later attempts to unseat him.

Her adopted country incorporated not only those territories in Eastern and Central France from which its name derived, but also a large area of Flanders, gained in earlier intermittent campaigns. During the prosecution of one of these expeditions, Charles the Bold had been killed in 1477, but Margaret continued to reside in Burgundy. She was a popular figure with most of her subjects, having compensated for her own lack of children by dutifully attending to the education of her four grandchildren. Furthermore, her substantial dowry, and efficient government, ensured that considerable financial reserves were always available.

Lincoln reached the Burgundian province of Brabant shortly after the arrival of Viscount Lovell. Both were welcomed by the fifty-one year old widow, who greeted the conspiracy with unbridled enthusiasm, whether or not she had actually helped to initiate the scheme. Although she had probably never seen Lambert Simnel, and knew (if only at second-hand) that the pretender was not her young nephew, she nevertheless accepted his claim. Henceforth, the Burgundian chronicler, Jean Molinet, referred to him as the Earl of Warwick.

There was another sterling service that she was able to perform for these warlike Yorkist noblemen. After a personal appeal to her son-in-law, Maximilian, King of the Romans, they were supplied with two thousand German mercenaries. Commanded by Colonel Martin Schwartz, a highly-experienced officer, these troops were strictly-disciplined, and well-armed with pikes and crossbows. They would form the backbone of the rebel army in the ensuing campaign.

The first leg of Lincoln's itinerary had been successfully completed. Now the time had arrived to unite the scattered elements of this Yorkist conspiracy, and complete the formalities surrounding

Simnel's claim. At the end of April, Lincoln, Lovell and their army of dour professionals, sailed off down the Channel. They were bound for Dublin, the focal point of the growing rebellion.

CHAPTER SIX

SPRING MANOEUVRES

*'He then came to the place called Walsingham,
where he prayed devoutly before the image of
the Blessed Virgin Mary, who is worshipped
with special devotion there, that he might be
preserved from the wiles of his enemies.'*

Polydore Vergil
'Anglica Historia'. (1534)

Both politically and militarily, Lincoln's defection was a terrible
blow to Henry VII. The rebels now had the support of an authentic
claimant to the throne, who would give even greater credibility to
the pretender Simnel. Lincoln would also be capable of replacing
him and inaugurating a strong, united Yorkist regime, at the appropriate time. Additionally, the apparent ease with which the
King had been duped by Lincoln, did little to enhance his
reputation for sound judgement.

The strategic implications of Lincoln's departure were, at first,
even more depressing. There seemed to be every prospect that
Henry would have to face that most unnerving of situations which
any supreme commander would wish to avoid — a war on two
fronts.

An invasion from Ireland, probably directed at the North-West
of England, to link up with Yorkist supporters there, was certainly
not to be treated lightly. In the short-term, however, it was the least
menacing of the two dangers. The rebels would land well over two
hundred miles from the capital, and would face a long, arduous
trek, either east through the Pennines, or south through the Welsh
Marches, before they posed a serious military threat.

In contrast, an invasion of Eastern England from Flanders
would require immediate attention. A mercenary force, led by Lincoln and Lovell, would have the benefits of flat terrain and
relatively good roads. The successful East coast invasions of Henry

Bolingbroke (1399) and Edward IV (1471), underlined the need for vigilance against any rebel force landing there.

The months of March and April were, inevitably, an anxious period for Henry. Characteristically, he refused to be idle. He did not expect an immediate invasion, but nevertheless he ordered musters of troops in both of the threatened areas, and appointed the two generals who would assume overall command when the incursions materialised.

In the North-West, military power was invested in his uncle, Jasper Tudor, Earl of Pembroke and first Duke of Bedford. Now nearly fifty-six years old, Jasper was the son of Owen Tudor and Catherine of France, the widow of Henry V. Jasper's elder brother, Edmund, Earl of Richmond, had died in 1456 before the birth of his son, Henry Tudor. Jasper had conscientiously assumed the role of guardian of his deceased brother's posthumously born child, and was devoted to his nephew's welfare. Another equally-loyal friend and supporter was given control of royal forces in the East of England. Here the commander was John de Vere, thirteenth Earl of Oxford, a forty-four year old veteran of the Wars of the Roses.

Both generals possessed several common attributes. They had both lost fathers, executed at the hands of the Yorkists. They had both, naturally, been unswerving in their allegiance to the Lancastrian cause in general, and Henry VII in particular, even sharing the difficult years of his exile in Brittany and France. Most important of all, they were both exceptionally experienced in the art of war. Jasper Tudor had defied Yorkist power for no less than seven years, during the siege of Harlech Castle (1461-68) on the west coast of Wales, only surrendering when the garrison had been reduced to an effective strength of fifty men. The Earl of Oxford was equally familiar with military campaigns. He had fought against Edward IV at Barnet (1471), had master-minded the short-lived capture of St. Michael's Mount in Cornwall (1473), and had commanded the most heavily-engaged wing of Henry's army at Bosworth Field. The selection of two such trusted and accomplished commanders, emphasised the King's concern over the impending crisis.

Having completed these preliminaries, Henry left London in March, at the head of a strong force, to conduct a Royal Progress of East Anglia, aimed at strengthening the loyalty of those counties most likely to be invaded by Lincoln and Lovell. Marching north-east to Bury St. Edmunds, he received news of the anxious approach of Thomas Grey, Marquess of Dorset.

A son of the disgraced Queen Dowager, by her first husband, the Lancastrian knight, Sir John Grey, Dorset had been an active supporter of Henry during Richard III's reign, and had fled to join him in Brittany after the failure of Buckingham's rebellion in 1484. He had not, however, taken part in the successful invasion of the following year, and had only recently been recalled to England by the King. His mother's sudden change of fortune horrified Dorset, particularly since accusations of his personal disloyalty were also being circulated, and he felt that an instant declaration of his fidelity to Henry VII would be his best hope of salvation.

Fortunately for him, the King had little cause to suspect a man who had shared his misfortunes and exile; indeed most of his senior advisers were from this source. In the present tense circumstances though, Henry believed that a close association with Dorset might be seen as a sign of weakness, and therefore sent the Earl of Oxford to intercept him and escort him to the Tower. Dorset was reassured that this was merely a temporary precaution to safeguard his own reputation, and the security of the King. Moreover, Henry promised to recompense him for this inconvenience when the present crisis had been resolved. Later, he was as good as his word, employing Dorset in many important civil and military capacities.

From Bury St. Edmunds, Henry moved on to Norwich, where he celebrated Easter, and then marched northwards via Fakenham to visit the famous shrine of Our Lady of Walsingham. This hallowed spot had been a place of pilgrimage since the reign of Edward the Confessor, when the Lord of the Manor's widow, Richeldis, had seen a vision of the Virgin Mary. Richeldis claimed that on three separate occasions her spirit had been transported to Nazareth, where Christ's mother had shown her the house in which the Angel Gabriel had appeared to her at the Annunciation, and had instructed the widow to note its measurements and build a reproduction in her own village. Faithful to her commandments, Richeldis had supervised the building of a wooden replica, erected in 1061. By the fifteenth century, this chapel was enclosed by a protective outer building, referred to as the novum opus.

The fame and reputation of Walsingham's shrine had grown steadily for more than four hundred years. Since the reign of Richard the Lionheart (1189-99), almost every King of England had paid at least one visit; Edward I (1272-1307) had been there thirteen times. Noblemen and beggars, saints and cut-throats, augmented the tens of thousands of common folk who devotedly trudged into

Walsingham each year. There, in the dark little chapel, illuminated only by tapers which reflected from walls encrusted with gold, silver, and jewels donated by grateful pilgrims, they prayed in gratitude for past favours or in expectation of future blessings.

Henry VII was no exception. The influence of his devout mother, Lady Margaret Beaufort, had instilled in him an obsession for the observation of religious forms, which bordered upon the superstitious. On disembarking near Milford Haven at the outset of his successful invasion in August, 1485, he had knelt on the beach and recited the psalm 'Judica me, Deus, et decerne causam meam', and later that month, after his victory at Bosworth Field, he had instructed that the 'Te Deum laudamus' should be sung in the presence of the whole army. Now, at Walsingham, sensing further dangers close at hand, Henry made the appropriate vows as he prayed for help and deliverance.

Having achieved his political and spiritual objectives, Henry turned south, passing through Cambridge and arriving back in London at the end of April. He had asserted his authority in an uncompromising fashion that would not be lost on friends, enemies, or neutrals. Yet, within days of his return, he would receive disturbing news. The rebels, he would learn, had concentrated their forces in one location, and a large-scale invasion of his realm was now imminent.

CHAPTER SEVEN

THE ZENITH OF THE REBELLION

'My Lords of Ireland, you will crown apes at last!'

King Henry VII, to a delegation of Irish peers. (1489)

The arrival in Dublin on May 5th of Lincoln, Lovell, Schwartz, and their two-thousand-strong force, had produced an electrifying effect upon the Irish Yorkists. Hitherto, they had been willing to proclaim Simnel as king, but had been more guarded about formalising his claim, or lending the military support needed to enforce it in England. The disembarkation of the impressive battle-hardened Germans, under the command of a colonel, who was likened by a contemporary chronicler to King Diomedes, the hero of the Trojan Wars, dispelled any lingering reservations they may have had. Immediately, the preparations for the boy's coronation, and the raising of an army, were put in hand.

For young Lambert Simnel, the weeks that followed marked the zenith of his brief, meteoric career, and it is to his credit that he executed the deception required of him with conviction and aplomb. On Whit Sunday, May 24th, he was escorted by his supporters to Christ Church Cathedral. Situated on a hill near the centre of Dublin, this magnificent building was already more that three hundred years old. Its construction had begun in 1172, just three years after the English invasion, and had taken fifty years to complete. The legendary ''Strongbow'' was buried there, and no church in Ireland was so symbolic of state authority.

With all due solemnity, Simnel was crowned King Edward VI with a diadem borrowed from a statue of the Virgin Mary, and an appropriate sermon was preached by John Payne, the Bishop of Meath. After all, these proceedings had been sanctioned by Walter Fitz Simmons, the Archbishop of Dublin who, like so many others, had been persuaded that Simnel's claim was authentic. The formalities having been completed, Simnel was seated on the shoulders of Darcy of Platten, the tallest man of his time in Ireland, and was shown to the crowds outside. An Irish parliament was summoned to mark the beginning of a new reign, and fresh coins were struck. The transformation from humble schoolboy to reigning monarch was momentarily complete.

There were a few isolated pockets of resistence. Although most of the Irish clergy had accepted Simnel's claim, two leading clergymen, the Bishop of Clogher, and the Archbishop of Armagh (a Florentine named Octavian de Palatio), refused to sanction the proceedings. It mattered little. Both were based in the North of the country, too far removed from the centre of the conspiracy to initiate widespread opposition. Similarly, a few towns in the South East, where Butler influence was strong — notably Kilkenny, Clonmel and Waterford — also refused to recognise the pretender, but could not muster the military resources necessary to take the field against the Yorkists and hinder their future plans.

Shortly after Simnel's coronation, Lincoln, Lovell and the Fitz Geralds, adopting the role of Council to their new king, met to discuss their next move. Basically, there were two courses open to them. The first was to remain in Ireland, mopping-up the token opposition to their recently-crowned figure-head, and flouting Henry VII's distant authority. This scheme was not without its advantages. If Henry could be lured across the Irish Sea, he would have to commit a significant force to subdue a largely hostile country, and during his absence, English Yorkists might prove capable of organizing risings against his government, similar in scale to those of 1486, but with a far greater chance of success.

This strategy had two serious drawbacks, of which finance was the most serious. Ireland was a poor country, in comparison with England, with a very limited revenue. The cost of maintaining two thousand mercenaries, for an indefinite period, was therefore prohibitive. Furthermore, the companies of beggarly Irish arriving in the capital in response to the Fitz Geralds' call to arms, were eager for immediate action. Numbering between four and six thousands, the enthusiastic courage of these troops was their main, if not their only, asset. They lacked experience, there having been no sizeable military operations in Ireland for a quarter of a century. Worse still, they were very poorly-equipped. A shortage of armour, in a country where it was not traditionally worn, left them unprotected against death or serious injury, and most were armed with little more than darts and long, Gaelic daggers. It was essential to deploy these men of mercurial temperament whilst they were still thirsting for action, fired by the prospect of booty and the satisfaction of installing their own king on the throne of their mighty neighbour.

The second option open to the rebel leaders was, therefore, to mount an immediate invasion of England. Once they had taken this step there would, of course, be no turning back, but still it seemed the most promising course of action, after several important factors had been considered. Their available forces probably already numbered between six and eight thousands, and were between three and four times as large as those landed by Henry Tudor in Wales, two years earlier. Indeed, the combined German and Irish contingents were actually more numerous than the five thousand-strong army with which Henry triumphed at Bosworth Field. Lovell was confident that a large Yorkist force would join the invaders in Lancashire under the command of Sir Thomas Broughton, and both he and Lincoln also believed that further detachments would rally to their cause elsewhere, especially in Yorkshire. Given their unbounded optimism, it is hardly surprising that in the ensuing campaign, Schwartz expressed his disgust at the way he had been misled on this issue, though he felt duty-bound to continue in their service. Finally, the rebel leaders were unduly influenced by the comparative ease with which they had succeeded in Ireland, and confidently expected the opposition in England to be easily reconciled or crushed, as circumstances would dictate.

In this ebullient mood, the rebel army, accompanied by Simnel, Symonds, Lincoln, Lovell and Thomas Fitz Gerald, embarked and set sail at the beginning of June. Their immediate objective was the coast of Lancashire, just over one hundred and thirty miles to the north-east. Their ultimate destination would, they believed, be London which they would enter in triumph before the end of the month. Few of their number, at this stage, could visualise the disappointments, rigours and final destruction that would beset their romantic but ill-conceived expedition.

CHAPTER EIGHT

CONVERGING COURSES

'But their snowball did not gather as it went,
for the people came not in to them, neither
did any rise or declare themselves in other
parts of the kingdom for them.'

Francis Bacon
'The History of the Reign of
Henry VII (1622)

When Henry VII returned to London at the end of April and
discovered that Lincoln and Lovell had taken their German mercenaries to Ireland, he had no option but to take the field again. He
accurately gauged that the rebel force would almost certainly land
on the West coast, probably in Lancashire, but at this stage he
could not afford to position his own army so far to the north. In
the event of an alternative invasion route being chosen, London
would be left largely unprotected, and its occupation by the rebels
would give them important psychological and practical advantages.

It was therefore strategically sound to take up a central position
in the Midlands, covering the major roads to the capital but
enabling the six thousand-strong royal army commanded by Oxford and Bedford to strike quickly at the invaders. By May 8th,
Henry had reached Kenilworth Castle, five miles to the south-east
of Coventry, an imposing Norman fortress enclosing seven acres
and dominating the small town which sheltered beneath its rampar-
ts. For a whole month his force would camp here, whilst the king
scoured intelligence reports from his spies, infiltrators, and supporters.

On June 4th, the rebel fleet reached the coast of North Lancashire and disembarked their army at the Piel of Foulney, a spit of
land situated near Furness Abbey. Their first disappointment oc-
curred soon after. Although the stalwart Sir Thomas Broughton
joined them immediately, he brought only a small company of
loyal Yorkists with him. With such a large proportion of their army

inadequately equipped, it was essential that significant numbers of heavily-armed, and preferably experienced, English supporters should join them. Throughout the campaign, these hopes never materialised.

Undeterred, Lincoln boldly marched his army south-eastwards through the Aire gap in the Pennines and on into Yorkshire; but the popular response did not improve. Indeed, it is doubtful if many more than a thousand English Yorkists joined them during the whole campaign.

Several reasons have been suggested for this indifference. Perhaps the most popular, is the assertion that the invaders consisted almost entirely of Germans and Irish, which restrained supporters among the insular English, who had a natural aversion towards a claimant who had to be carried to the throne on the backs of foreigners. This explanation is, on balance, unconvincing. Both Edward IV (1471) and Henry VII (1485) had invaded with forces which consisted almost exclusively of foreign mercenaries, yet each had been able to recruit thousands of men in various parts of England and Wales. Furthermore, although the bulk of the rebel army was composed of impoverished and ill-clad Irishmen, it did little to alienate the local population in the Northern shires. On the contrary, it is to the credit of the rebel leaders that, if only for tactical reasons, they maintained firm discipline throughout and prevented their men from harrassing civilians along their line of march — no mean feat, considering the motivation of most of the Irish.

There were other important reasons why English sympathisers held back. One was a reservation, if not downright resentment, felt towards Lovell in the aftermath of the abortive rising of the previous year, followed by his subsequent flight. Another, was a grudging respect for Henry VII as a firm and energetic ruler, who had already shown himself capable of dealing with opposition quickly and efficiently.

By the time the rebels reached York, the weakness of their position was apparent. Their numbers had not increased appreciably, there had been no risings anywhere else in the country in support of Simnel, and Henry had now left Kenilworth and was moving against them. In this increasingly isolated position, Lincoln believed that the only practical way to maintain the initiative was to search out the royal army and bring it to battle at once. A single, decisive victory now offered him the best chance of success. This was by no means impossible given the unpredictable nature of fifteenth century warfare, and the considerable fighting ability of the German mercanaries. Schwartz, although disillusioned by the exaggerated predictions of his superiors, felt duty-bound to support their latest desperate gamble. Stolidly, the rebel army marched south towards the strategically important town of Newark, which Lincoln intended to capture and use as a base.

News of the invasion had reached Henry VII within a few days of the landing. Meticulous as ever, he had sent a trusted friend to inspect the Lancashire coast before the rebels had even arrived. Sir Christopher Urswick, Henry's Chaplain and Confessor, had been in the service of the king and his mother for many years, and was regularly employed on diplomatic missions. His current task had been to discover which ports were capable of handling large ships, so that detachments of the royal army could hinder, if not prevent, the disembarkation of the rebel forces. Returning from this commission, Urswick heard that the landing near Furness had been effected, and sent a messenger ahead to inform the king immediately.

The military crisis now about to break, must have caused Henry to reflect upon his complete reversal of role, compared with the Bosworth campaign less than two years earlier. Then, it had been Richard III who had controlled a numerically-superior force in the centre of England, waiting to smite down an outnumbered, upstart invader. Now that Henry himself was in that favoured position, he did not underestimate either the enemy, or the possibility that a combination of treachery and inertia could upset his best laid plans. He was determined to confront the rebels only if morale in his own army was high, and if he could rely on those officers and men who would have to bear the brunt of the fighting.

Marching out of Kenilworth, his troops passed through Coventry (June 8th), Wigston Parva (June 9th), Leicester (June 10th), and Loughborough (June 11th), arriving at the village of Bunny, barely six miles south of Nottingham on the evening of June 12th. The next day — Wednesday, June 13th — the advance guard of the royal army crossed the bridge over the River Trent and entered the town, whilst the king kept the bulk of his forces on the south bank, probably near the village of Clifton, though some detachments may have camped in the neighbouring villages of Wilford and Ruddington.

At this crucial juncture, Henry's confidence was boosted by the numerous contingents of troops, which were pouring in to join him from many different parts of the country. Their commanders included George Talbot, fourth Earl of Shrewsbury, the nineteen year old grandson of one of England's legendary heroes from the Hundred Years' War against the French; Sir John Cheney, a knight renowned for his immense physical strength, who had fought in Henry's personal bodyguard at Bosworth Field; and at least seventy other knights and gentlemen, who were either obeying the royal summons or offering their services voluntarily.

On the morning of Thursday, June 14th, whilst his entire army marched into Nottingham, Henry observed Corpus Christi day by attending divine service in the town, probably at St. Mary's Church. Shortly afterwards, he was delighted to receive a strong body of troops from Lancashire, commanded by Lord Strange, the brother of Sir William Stanley, whose decisive charge had clinched Henry's victory at Bosworth Field. Strange had himself been held hostage by Richard III during that campaign, and had nearly been executed during the battle when his father, Thomas Stanley, first Earl of Derby, had refused to support Richard in his hour of need. With the arrival of Strange's companies, the royal army had roughly doubled in strength since its departure from Kenilworth a week earlier, and now numbered about twelve thousand men.

That night, it presented an awesome sight as it spread across the fields and meadows just to the south of the town and its castle. From Lenton in the west, to the town bridge over the River Leen in the east, was congregated an exceptionally powerful army, probably even larger than that assembled by Richard III two years before. Its sojourn in Nottingham was destined to be a short one.

The king had been monitoring the progress of the rebel army, partly by sending a troop of light horsemen to capture stragglers, but also by planting spies in their midst. Whilst at Nottingham, having received the news that his enemies were heading towards Newark, he promptly called a Council of War, to consider whether to advance against the rebels, or play a waiting game. The former course was favoured, not least by the king himself. Morale in his rapidly-expanding army was high, but he also feared (unnecessarily) that any delay might encourage greater support for his enemies.

Determined to intercept the rebels before they could reach their objective, the royal army left Nottingham on Friday, June 15th. Re-crossing Trent bridge, they set off eastwards along the south bank of the river, heading for the Fosse Way, the ancient Roman road, which would lead them directly into Newark. Their progress was slow, and the atmosphere tense. A rumour that the rebels were near and about to attack, caused a sudden wave of panic, but the experienced Oxford quickly restored order, and led the army on towards the villages of Radcliffe-on-Trent and Holme Pierrepoint, where they bivouaced for the night.

The rebel army was, indeed, very close at hand. On that same evening, having marched through Southwell, Lincoln's forces had approached the north bank of the River Trent. Newark Castle was garrisoned by troops loyal to Henry VII, but an unguarded crossing-point was available at Fiskerton, four miles to the south-west of the town. Here, the river was easily fordable in mid-summer, and the rebel army crossed to the south bank, and occupied positions on the rising ground astride the Fosse Way, close to the villages of East Stoke and Elston.

The rival armies, probably totalling twenty-one thousand men, were now approximately ten miles apart, most of which could be traversed by a good, direct road. Both were commanded by leaders who had committed themselves to a decisive victory and had everything to gain or lose from the outcome. The scene was set for a protracted and sanguinary contest, which would only end with the utter destruction of either of the protagonists.

CHAPTER NINE

THE BATTLE OF STOKE FIELD

'Concerning this battle the relations that are
left unto us are so naked and negligent,
though it be an action of so recent memory,
that they rather declare the success of the
day than the manner of the fight.'

> Francis Bacon
> *'The History of the Reign of*
> *King Henry VII'. (1622)*

'The following day the king, having formed
his whole force into three columns, marched
to the village of Stoke, halted before the
earl's camp and, on the level ground there,
offered battle. Accepting the chance, the
earl led forward his troops and, at a given
signal, gave battle. Both sides fought with
the bitterest energy.'

> Polydore Vergil
> *'Anglica Historia'. (1534)*

'... the victory whereof fell unto the king,
loved by God, how be it that by subtle ways men
were set atween the place of the field and many
of the king's subjects which were coming toward
his Grace, showing unto them that the king had
lost the field and was fled.'

> *'The Great Chronicle of London'*

When Henry VII arose on the morning of Saturday, June 16th,

he conscientiously heard two masses in preparation for the trials and tribulations he expected to face that day. His army was ordered to break camp at about six o'clock, and soon reached the Fosse Way, guided by five local men from Radcliffe. Though ignorant of the exact position of the rebel army, the king had prepared his forces for action. The intrepid Oxford led the vanguard, in full array, some distance in advance of the two other, slightly smaller divisions or "battles". Oxford's force, composed largely of infantry and archers but strengthened by heavily-armoured cavalry on each wing, accounted for between a third and a half of the royal army.

Once on to the Fosse Way, their progress was rapid, and by nine o'clock that morning, the rebel army could be seen, less than a mile ahead, occupying strong defensive positions on either side of the road. Oxford's men were now probably just to the north of the hamlet of Elston Towers, whilst the second and third "battles" were lagging about a mile behind, in the vicinity of Syerston.

The exact dispositions of the rebel army are very difficult to establish, but were likely to have been influenced by the local terrain, and also by the nationality of the men involved. It would have made sound tactical sense for them to occupy the higher ground on either side of the Fosse Way. This would entail placing their left wing between Stoke and Elston, to the east of the road; their centre to the west of Stoke village, on the knoll overlooking the Trent; and their right wing between Stoke and the river bank.

Problems over language also had to be handled carefully, and considerable autonomy would have had to be devolved upon German and Irish officers, despite Lincoln's theoretical position of overall command. It seems likely that he placed the bulk of Thomas Fitz Gerald's large Irish contingent on the left; although this gave his line of battle a lop-sided appearance, these poorly-armed men had few advantages, other than raw courage and superior numbers. The centre was held by Schwartz's Germans who, by contrast, were moderate in numbers, but well-armed and highly professional. Finally, the right was probably composed of the small English company, augmented by some Irishmen, and commanded by Lovell and Broughton.

Details about the course of the battle of Stoke Field, as it later came to be known, are exceptionally sparse. The chroniclers wrote such terse and unsatisfactory accounts, that they have justifiably been accused of negligence, and an unwillingness to record anything, other than the result. In the absence of a precise tactical appreciation, posterity has had to be satisfied with a bare outline of

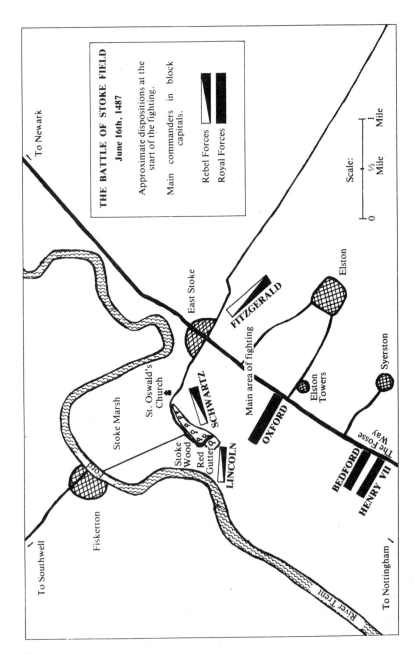

THE BATTLE OF STOKE FIELD
June 16th, 1487

Approximate dispositions at the start of the fighting.

Main commanders in block capitals.

Rebel Forces
Royal Forces

Scale:
0   ½   1
     Mile Mile

To Newark

To Southwell

Fiskerton

Stoke Marsh

East Stoke

St. Oswald's Church

Stoke Wood

Red Gutter

LINCOLN

SCHWARTZ

FITZGERALD

Main area of fighting

Elston

Elston Towers

OXFORD

Syerston

The Fosse Way

BEDFORD

HENRY VII

River Trent

To Nottingham

the main events.

As soon as Lincoln saw the royal army, in all its splendour, marching towards his position, he realised that he had to take the initiative. Given the numerical superiority of the enemy, Lincoln hoped to attack and repel the vanguard, before the two other royal "battles" could come to its aid. The rebels were soon advancing quickly down the gently sloping ground to assail Oxford's men in the large, unenclosed fields on either side of the Fosse Way.

After exchanging volleys of arrows and crossbow bolts, the rival armies became locked in the typically savage hand-to-hand combat with sword, mace, battle-axe and pike, which was so common during the Wars of the Roses. For nearly three hours this merciless carnage continued unabated, a remarkably long period of time to sustain close-quarter fighting. This phenomenon is easily explained. Most of the rebel troops were foreigners, who had little hope of clemency if they surrendered, and few prospects of finding refuge if they fled. Their commitment to victory was hardened by dire necessity.

Without exception, the chroniclers applauded the courage and obstinacy of all the rebel forces, but identified the Germans as the most formidable. Schwartz was held to have few equals among Englishmen in either bravery, strength, or prowess, whilst his men had, it was claimed, been toughened by regular and arduous physical training. Contemporary opinion even went so far as to suggest that the real danger to the Tudor dynasty at Stoke Field, came from the Germans. References to Schwartz and his men appeared in several popular songs of the period, and also in the works of the satirical poet, John Skelton (c. 1460 to 1529). Some of these were passed on to later generations by Sir Walter Scott in his novel "Kenilworth" (1821). For the moment, though as long as these daunting German formations remained intact, the rebels had some hope of victory.

At one point, this nearly materialised. With no clear advantage having been gained by either side, ugly rumours began to circulate in the second and third "battles" of the royal army, claiming that the king had fled and his vanguard had been routed. These malicious lies also appear to have spread to the rear of the royal forces, deterring many late arrivals from joining the reserve divisions, commanded by Henry and his uncle, Bedford. If these dilatory forces had been nearer to the actual fighting, their hasty departure could have had disastrous consequences. However, since they had hung back in a position of relative safety, their fears were not communicated to the front-line troops, and the crisis passed. Referring to this matter, in a letter to Pope Innocent VIII a few weeks later (July 5th, 1487), Henry clearly regarded the ruse in the most serious light, believing it to be an invention of the faint-hearted and disloyal, who thus attempted to conceal their own failure to support him decisively.

Towards mid-day, Oxford's vanguard began to gain the upper hand. The left-wing of the rebel army was probably the first to succumb. Casualties among the unprotected Irishmen had been so heavy that the fighting here had resembled a massacre rather than a battle, and the dwindling number of survivors were gradually forced back behind the centre and right of the rebel line. Disheartened by the fearful destruction of their comrades-in-arms, the Germans and the English Yorkists were also finally broken by a decisive charge from the royal army. Whether this was executed with the assistance of reinforcements from the second and third "battles", or by the heavy cavalry on the wings of the vanguard, is open to question; but its impact was not. Resistance along the rebel line disintegrated, and they attempted to flee back towards Fiskerton ferry, which they had crossed the previous evening.

The situation contained all the ingredients for a disaster. Behind their backs was a sharp defile, later called the "Red Gutter". Along this congested track, many of the fugitives would be cut down by the victors. Those among the rebels who successfully negotiated this hazard, were still in desperate peril. Hemmed in on three sides by the river, they had to retreat across the area known as Stoke Marsh for over three-quarters of a mile before reaching the ford. Very few would have been able to avail themselves of the narrow footpath, and in their exhausted state they were easy prey for their pursuers. Many undoubtedly reached the Trent and swam or waded to the temporary safety of its northern bank, but not before at least half of the rebel army had been hacked to death or taken prisoner.

At least six thousand men had perished in this dour struggle, possibly between five and six times as many as at Bosworth Field. Two thousand of Oxford's heavily engaged vanguard were dead, and a large, but unspecified, number had been wounded. Among the four thousand rebel dead were virtually all the major leaders, including the Earl of Lincoln, Thomas Fitz Gerald, Martin Schwartz, and Sir Thomas Broughton. All had led by example, fighting with dogged determination and refusing any opportunity of flight. They had made the supreme sacrifice for the cause they had so enthusiastically espoused.

Lincoln's death in battle was a bitter disappointment to Henry VII. He had hoped that the "Dark Earl" would be taken alive, since a thorough interrogation might have revealed the real aim of the rebellion, and its full complement of supporters. The haul of prisoners was not, however, totally devoid of leaders. The pretender and his tutor had both been captured. Simnel had no doubt been spared during the slaughter on account of his youth, and Symonds because of his clerical status. Both now awaited the punishments which their tragic acts of folly had earned.

A sole possible survivor from the upper echelons of the rebellion, may have been Lord Lovell. His body was not discovered on the field of battle; on the contrary, there were reports that he had been seen in full flight. Several legends surround his disappearance. He may have been killed or drowned whilst crossing the Trent, or attempting to scramble up the steep bank on the far side. Alternatively, he may have escaped altogether and gone into hiding, protected by relatives and servants, at either Rotherfield Greys, near Henley, or Minster Lovell, near Witney in Oxfordshire. Many years later, in 1708, a secret vault was discovered at Lovell's house in the latter village. It contained a skeleton, seated at a table with writing materials and a book, and many have assumed this to be the remains of the Viscount, who had accidently starved to death, after his guardian had either died or had been killed or imprisoned by a search party. Whatever the fate of this diehard Yorkist, Henry VII had rid himself of an obdurate and dangerous enemy.

As the king surveyed Stoke Field on the afternoon of June 16th, his feelings were those of relief rather than elation. Although he had little enthusiasm for war, and had certainly never regarded the outcome of this campaign as a foregone conclusion, he no doubt greeted the victory with a grim satisfaction. There was, however, still much to be done. Until he had taken every precaution to publicise the end of the rebellion, and ensure that further attempts were more difficult to initiate, he could not afford to rest on his laurels.

CHAPTER TEN

MOPPING—UP—OPERATIONS

'Lambert the false boy king was indeed captured,
with his mentor Richard: but each was granted
his life — the innocent lad because he was too
young to have committed any offence, the tutor
because he was a priest.'

> Polydore Vergil
> 'Anglica Historia'. (1534)

'The queen was with great solemnity crowned at
Westminster, the five and twentieth of November,
in the third year of his reign, which was about
two years after the marriage; like an old
christening, that had stayed long for godfathers.'

> Francis Bacon
> 'The History of the Reign of
> King Henry VII.' (1622)

Even before his departure from Stoke Field, Henry had almost certainly decided upon the fate of his two most troublesome captives. It was a traditional practice, during the Wars of the Roses, to execute important prisoners without delay, and this custom had already been upheld by the king after Bosworth Field, when Sir William Catesby, one of Richard III's right-hand men, had been executed just two days later in Leicester. On this occasion, however, Henry had devised more appropriate punishments.

Simnel fared the best. The king had long realised that the pretender was merely a puppet, cynically manipulated by others, and therefore deserving mercy. Henry also wished to avoid being stigmatised as a murderer or gaoler of children. The Earl of Warwick's fate was a sufficient liability already. Instead, by keeping

Simnel alive and employing him in a menial capacity, Henry could emphasise the boy's humble origins, pour scorn on those who had supported him, and deter other pretenders with a living spectacle of the ridiculous fate they would encounter. So, by an ironic twist of fate, the child who briefly dominated national affairs, who had been crowned as a king in Ireland, and had acted as the catalyst for a major invasion of England, was now set to work as a turnspit in the royal kitchens.

No doubt he adapted to his complete change of status without deep resentment, because he was later promoted from scullion to the post of Royal Falconer, and was eventually transferred to the household of Sir Thomas Lovell. This stalwart Lancastrian, a veteran of Bosworth and Stoke Field, held a wide range of senior offices under both Henry VII and his son, Henry VIII. Simnel appears to have served at Lovell's family seat at Elsing in Middlesex, at least until the death of his new-found master, whose magnificent funeral at Shoreditch he probably attended in 1525. Little is known about Simnel's final years, but he may have been alive as late as 1534, and could have been the father of Richard Simnel, the canon of St. Osith's in Essex at the Dissolution of the Monasteries.

If Henry's treatment of Simnel was pervaded by a spirit of watchful paternalism, then the savage punishment of Symonds reflected the more ruthless side of his character. After the meddlesome priest had been questioned, he was packed off to a dungeon for the rest of his life, and heard of no more. The king could not authorise his execution, even on a charge of treason, without committing him for trial. If he infringed the right of benefit of clergy in this way, he risked a rift with the Pope, whose co-operation he was currently seeking. Since Henry had no desire to permit a trial, his attitude tends to strengthen the view that the Queen Dowager was a major force in the conspiracy. Symonds testimony would have shattered the facade of reconciliation between the houses of York and Lancaster, which the king was striving to sustain.

Having dealt with this pair of wretched miscreants, Henry VII departed from the scene of his hard-won victory, and continued his march along the Fosse Way to Lincoln, twenty miles north-east of the battlefield. In this ancient city, from which the "Dark Earl's" title had derived, Henry offered prayers of thanksgiving in the magnificent Norman Cathedral. Afterwards, the royal banner, emblazoned with the Red Dragon of Cadwallader, was despatched to the shrine at Walsingham as a final token of his devotion and gratitude for his recent deliverance.

Throughout the rest of the summer, Henry conducted a royal progress of the north of England. Comparatively few Englishmen had joined the invaders or aided them, but nevertheless the king was vindictive towards the minority who had. With a large army at his disposal, and ample justification to visit the north, this was a good opportunity to re-assert his authority. As his forces marched through Pontefract and York, towards Durham, anyone suspected of having sympathised with the rebellion was either arrested or summoned. After a strict inquisition, the majority were fined; this was not the last occasion on which this finance-conscious king would force his opponents to defray the costs of his campaigns.

The northern limit of the progress was Newcastle, where Henry rested his army for five days in mid-August. From this convenient location, he despatched two ambassadors across the border to Edinburgh in an attempt to improve relations with Scotland, and deny his enemies a base from which to operate. His hopes were soon dashed. Although Richard Fox, his Principal Secretary and Lord Privy Seal, and Sir Richard Edgecombe, the Comptroller of the King's Household, were both mature and accomplished diplomats, the circumstances surrounding their mission made success unlikely. James III of Scotland received them courteously enough, and appeared to want peace, but his powerful nobility did not. Rather than incur their displeasure, he would only conclude a seven-year truce, which he privately promised to renew from time to time. Even this small gain proved worthless, for James was killed by rebel noblemen the following year, and replaced by his fifteen-year old son, James IV, who later supported Perkin Warbeck, another pretender to the English throne.

If the overtures to Scotland represented a diplomatic defeat, Henry was compensated to some extent by the great success of another mission, concluded in the same month. A Papal Bull, issued by Innocent VIII on August 6th, markedly strengthened Henry's internal security.

The popularity of this new pope had been flagging badly since his coronation in 1484. Having called for a crusade against the Turks, he had received a poor response, and would soon be bought off by a pension from the Sultan. His eternal meddling in Italian politics, and his lack of private morals, also ensured that he was increasingly regarded in the Christian world as lazy and unworthy. Henry VII realised that a little flattery might pay handsome dividends, and after his ambassador to Rome had greeted the Pope in suitably sycophantic terms, Innocent VIII was willing to assist one of his

few admirers by amending the privilege of sanct_____
portant ways.

Under the new laws, anyone availing themselves____
forfeited the ownership of all their property in the ou___
they had sought sanctuary after committing acts of____
king could appoint guardians to watch over them. Mos___
of all, if they left the sanctuary and performed further___
they lost the right forever. These measures related direc_____ .ie
recent activities of Lovell, the Staffords and others, and were a
powerful deterrent to disenchanted Yorkists.

It was a far more confident Henry VII who marched south from
Newcastle in the late summer and autumn of 1487, slowly
dismissing his forces en route, and entering London in triumph on
November 3rd, after an absence of six months. At the second
parliament of his reign, just six days later, no fewer than twenty-
eight of Simnel's former supporters were attainted. Yet there still
remained two outstanding problems which needed to be resolved
before the rebellion could be completely dismissed.

The recent crisis had convinced him that the coronation of his
wife was an essential measure to appease the House of York, and
on November 25th this long overdue ceremony was finally concluded. Elizabeth had been brought down the Thames from
Greenwich the day before, accompanied by her mother-in-law, and
had been warmly greeted by her husband in the royal apartments at
the Tower of London. On the day of the coronation, she was transported through the city to Westminster, along streets which were
hung with tapestries, silks, gold velvet and the liveries of craft
guilds. Sitting on the royal litter, and greeted at regular intervals by
choirs of children dressed as angels and virgins, the resplendent
young queen wore a gown and mantle of white cloth of gold, edged
with ermine, which enhanced her fair hair and pale complexion.

The ceremony was conducted by Archbishop Morton, whilst the
king and his mother looked on from a specially constructed plat-
form between the pulpit and high altar. Every effort was made to
extract the maximum propaganda value from the proceedings, by
emphasising the unity between York and Lancaster and the aban-
donment of rival claims to the throne. Although Elizabeth's
mother, the disgraced Queen Dowager, was not present, Henry's
wife was supported by her sister Cecily, her cousin Margaret, the
sister of the imprisoned Earl of Warwick, and her aunt Elizabeth,
mother of the deceased Earl of Lincoln. For good measure, the

ELIZABETH OF YORK, Artist unknown.
National Portrait Gallery

"Dark Earl's" father, and his younger brother Edmund, were also present. After three days of festivities, supervised by the Duke of Bedford, and concluded with a traditional banquet, Henry could feel well-pleased with his attempts to reconcile himself with his former enemies.

A further problem which had been illuminated by the Simnel conspiracy was less easy to remedy. Despite the death of Thomas Fitz Gerald and so many of his foolhardy recruits at Stoke Field, Ireland still remained under Yorkist control, and the Lord Deputy, Gerald Fitz Gerald, was too powerful to be summarily punished. Unwilling to authorise a penalty which he could not easily enforce, Henry sent Sir Richard Edgecombe to Dublin the following year to pardon the Earl of Kildare in return for his future co-operation.

The uneasy rapprochement did not last long. By 1491, Kildare was again under suspicion for helping the new pretender, Perkin Warbeck, and Henry had to resort to more stringent measures. These entailed the despatch of Sir Edward Poynings to Ireland as the king's new Lord Deputy in 1494 and 1495. Kildare was attainted and escorted to England as a prisoner to spend two years in the Tower. At last he learned his lesson. Pardoned, and reinstated as Lord Deputy in 1496, he married the king's cousin soon after his release and thereafter served loyally under both Henry VII and Henry VIII, until his death in 1513.

During his imprisonment, though, his autonomous powers had been reduced considerably. Under Poyning's Law (1494), the Irish parliament had effectively lost its independence. All future meetings and legislation had to be approved by the King of England and his council, an unhappy state of affairs which would prove a source of friction between the two nations for nearly three centuries.

With a few exceptions, Henry VII had exploited his victory at Stoke Field to the full, and by the end of 1487, he could devote his undivided attention to other affairs of state. Eager to impress upon his subjects the strength and permanence of his dynasty, it was naturally in his interests to minimise the challenge to his authority which he had warded off, and create the impression that his earlier victory at Bosworth Field had ushered in a period of successful and tranquil rule.

Inevitably, with the passage of time, the Simnel conspiracy and the battle of Stoke Field would be dismissed as trivial affairs, which had posed no substantial threat to the mighty Tudors, and deserved scant attention from the serious historian. Thus, by default, a major crisis in England's national history was either denigrated or wholly neglected.

CHAPTER ELEVEN

AN ASSESSMENT

'Now civil wounds are stopp'd, peace lives again:
That she may long live here, God say amen!'

William Shakespeare
'King Richard III' Act V; Scene V.

Despite the judgments of a wide range of prestigious literary figures and historians, from William Shakespeare to Sir Winston Churchill, the traditional claim that the battle of Bosworth Field marks the end of the Wars of the Roses, is regarded with growing sceptism by modern historians. Simultaneously, the Simnel conspiracy in general, and the battle of Stoke Field in particular, have been re-appraised in a more positive manner. This does not devalue the importance of Bosworth, which ended nearly a quarter of a century of Yorkist power and brought the first of the Tudor monarchs to the throne. Yet the increasingly accepted view that Stoke Field was the final Roses battle is very hard for the impartial and investigative historian to refute.

There were several remarkable similarities between the two battles. Both were preceded by sea-borne invasions of foreign and mercenary forces, both were the climax of arduous campaigns, and both were plagued by acts of treachery and deception. However, in three important aspects, Stoke Field was a far more formidable encounter. First, the numbers of men deployed on the field and committed to action by their commanders, was higher; secondly, the fighting was far more intense, and was sustained over a long period of time; and finally, the number of fatalities was many times greater.

After 1487, the Wars of the Roses did not conveniently end at a mathematical line. Abortive risings, skimishes and isolated sieges would continue for another ten years, and the instigator of many of these, the pretender Perkin Warbeck, is considered by many historians to have been a far greater menace to Henry VII than the misguided Lambert Simnel.

In some respects, this is a sound argument. Warbeck, a native of Tournai in Flanders, who claimed to be Edward IV's son, Richard of York, the younger of the Princes in the Tower, had several important advantages over Simnel. Born probably in 1475, he was significantly older than the Oxford schoolboy when he made his several bids for power between 1491 and 1497. He was at least as accomplished as an impersonator, infinitely more autonomous of manipulative Yorkists, and sufficiently convincing to enlist widespread diplomatic recognition. Whereas Simnel had only been assisted in Burgundy and Ireland, Warbeck at various times had the additional support of James IV of Scotland, the Holy Roman Emperor Maximillian I, and the French court.

Nevertheless, his four military incursions were all short-lived and ended in dismal failure. At Deal in 1495, the two to three hundred men he dared to put ashore were mopped up with contemptuous ease. Moving on to Ireland later that summer, although he was able to field an army of several thousands, his forces could neither capture the town of Waterford nor even maintain its siege for more than eleven days. The following year, his Scottish allies spent a mere two days on English soil in pursuit of his claim before retiring back across the Tweed. Last of all, his attempt to exploit Cornish grievances after their rising in 1497, was a final ignominious debacle. The poorly-armed rabble who rallied to him, estimated variously at between three and eight thousands, were unable to capture Exeter (or even inflict casualties upon its garrison), and melted away at the approach of royal forces.

None of these ventures ever developed to the stage where Henry could have been challenged in a pitched battle. This is highly significant. At Stoke Field, a defeat for Henry VII, even if not accompanied by his death or capture, would have had serious political repercussions. By contrast, none of Warbeck's expeditions ever did more than puncture the outer defences of the Tudor state. Naturally, the imprisonment of Warbeck in 1497, enabled Henry to breathe a profound sigh of relief, and with the execution of the pretender and his latest dupe, the miserable young Earl of Warwick, in 1499 the Tudor political edifice was complete. Yet, stressful though these alarms and threats to Henry's authority must have been, they never forced him to risk his crown on the result of a single battle. After June, 1487, the ultimate test for the Tudor dynasty was never applied again.

The battle of Stoke Field therefore represents a parting of the ways between the sordid dynastic feuds of the Wars of the Roses, and the more stable, rational, and orderly government of the Tudor era. It was at Stoke Field that Henry destroyed the most serious military threat to his rule, at a time when it was not firmly established. After the victory he was no longer a political adventurer, but a king recognised by other sovereigns. After his death in 1509, his successors would be held in equal esteem. Furthermore, the lessons he absorbed before and after the battle, urged him to hasten the process of political reconciliation which would make such crises far less likely to re-occur. For those reasons, the Simnel Conspiracy and the battle of Stoke Field are of far-reaching historical significance, and merit an acknowledged place in English history.

MAJOR SOURCES

PRIMARY SOURCES

Bernard Andre - *'Vita Henrici VII'* in Memorial of King Henry VII; ed. J. Gairdner, Rolls series (1858)
Great Chronicle of London - ed. A.H. Thomas and I.D. Thornley, London (1938)
Edward Hall - *Union of the Two Illustre Families of Lancaster and York* - ed. H. Ellis — London (1809)
Ingulph's Chronicle of the Abbey of Croyland, trans. and ed. H.T. Riley — London (1854)
Paston Letters, 1422-1509, ed. J. Gairdner — London (1904)
'The Song of Lady Bessy' in English Historical Literature in the Fifteenth Century — C.L. Kingsford — Oxford (1913)
The Anglica Historia of Polydore Vergil, A.D. 1485-1573 — trans and ed. D. Hay — Camden series (1950)

SECONDARY SOURCES

F. Bacon — *The History of the Reign of King Henry VII* — Folio Society (1971)
R. Brooke - *Visits to fields of battle in England in the fifteenth century* (1857)
S.B. Chrimes — *Henry VII* — Eyre Methuen (1972)
W.S. Churchill — *A History of the English-Speaking Peoples;* Vol. 3 — Cassell (1956)
A.E. Conway — *Henry VII, Relations with Scotland and Ireland 1485-1498* — Cambridge University Press (1932)
The Dictionary of National Biography — Oxford University Press (1917)
E. Jenkins — *The Princes in the Tower* — Hamish Hamilton (1978)
J.R. Lander — *The Wars of the Roses* — White Lion (1965)
R. Lockyer — *Henry VII* — Longman (1968)
D. MacGibbon — *Elizabeth Woodville* — London (1938)
J.D. Mackie — *The Earlier Tudors, 1485-1558* — Oxford University Press (1952)

A.Plowden — *The House of Tudor* — Weidenfield and Nicholson (1976)

C.D. Ross — *The Wars of the Roses* __ Thames and Hudson (1976)

D. Seward — *Richard III: England's Black Legend* — Country Life Books (1983)

R.L. Storey — *The Reign of Henry VII* — Blandford (1968)

P. Warner — *British Battlefields: The South* — Osprey (1972)

N. Williams — *The Life and Times of Henry VII* — Weidenfield and Nicholson (1973)

A. Williamson — *The Mystery of the Princes: An Investigation into a Supposed Murder* — Sutton (1978)

A.C. Wood — *A History of Nottinghamshire* — S.R. (1971)